Marc Lipman

I0472687

Photo Phinishing

By Marc Lipman

This book helps the amateur picture taker (aren't we all?) deal with the pictures that they have taken. It covers topics such as editing your pictures, organizing your pictures, and displaying your pictures

(I took 300 pictures of my week on LBI; Now what do I do with them?)

Photo Phinishing

Contents

Marc Lipman

Photo Phinishing

Introduction

Taking digital pictures is a common part of everyday life. Most of us do it. But not all of us know some of the simple tricks and techniques we can use once we have taken them.

To begin with, I am not a professional photographer. But I am a retired computer systems developer and a college professor. In addition, I have taken a number of excursions around the world and have children and grandchildren (lots of pictures). I believe this qualifies me to talk about this subject.

This book is NOT about taking pictures. It is about what to do after you have taken them. It is also NOT an instruction manual. It does NOT give you step-by-step instructions on how to do everything. It gives you ideas and concepts. If you want details, there is the Internet.

There are many topics that could have been covered in more detail. If the topic was beyond the scope of this book, I stated that the topic was beyond the scope of this book. If the topic is one that I don't know about, I state that the topic is beyond the scope of this book.

Since this involves computer devices and software (programs and apps to you), you should remember that things are constantly changing, and I will be lucky if there have not been a number of new and enhanced devices and programs by the time you read this. When I use the term "PC", I am referring to PC's and laptops, whether using Microsoft Windows, Linux, or MAC.

Another consideration is: ~~One Size Fits All~~ – WRONG! When I have a class of 25 students, there are often 25 answers as to how to take care of their pictures. You have to consider your own personal situation before coming up with solutions. One size does NOT fit all.

When I thought about writing a book about this subject, I wondered how long it should be. Then I decided I would start writing and stop when I was done covering the subjects. It is a little like sculpting a statue of a horse. You start with a chunk of granite and remove everything that does not look like a horse.

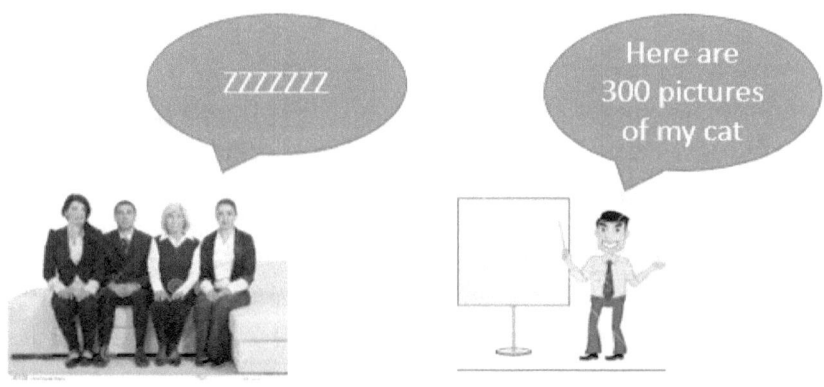

Photo Phinishing

Evolution

In the evolution of animals, we went from ancient sea creatures, to primitive animals that walked the earth, to the dinosaurs that were huge but not so smart, to mammals like us that were more reasonably sized and more intelligent.

In the evolution of digital photography, a similar evolution occurred. I remember telling film photographers that digital cameras would take over – they laughed at me. Now a film camera is a dinosaur (try to get film for one or get the film developed, it isn't easy).

The first digital cameras were toys with low resolution (.3 megapixel) and few features. The ways of showing your results were similarly primitive. Some TV's could be connected to your computer (if you had the proper cables) and the TV's of the time had smaller screens (a 31" screen was a large one).

They evolved. Where human evolution took millions of years, digital camera evolution took about 20 years. But like human evolution, we can only guess what the future holds.

Backups

My first important topic is Backups, because it is a very important (and sometimes forgotten) part of handling pictures. Many people are familiar with taking pictures using a number of devices: Cell phones, iPads, digital cameras as well as some other devices such as eyeglasses and binoculars. They are even familiar with backing up their pictures to their PC (and maybe even to the Cloud).

However, most people are not diligent enough when it comes to backing up their pictures (until it's too late).

Here is a real situation from a person. "I backed all my important pictures to my PC and erased them from my camera. Now my PC won't start. Help!" Fortunately, I was able to get her computer started. But what if I couldn't? Many of those pictures were of her deceased husband. Was I supposed to bring him back to life?

Or another one: "My pictures were on my PC at the shore house which Hurricane Sandy covered with four feet of water." Was I supposed to perform artificial respiration on a computer?

Or yet another one: "A tree fell on my house. My laptop and external hard drive are now pancakes." Should I get out the maple syrup?

The more important your pictures (and other data) are, the more important backups are. There are a number of approaches that you can take. If you only have a few pictures, a CD, DVD, or flash drive will do. Otherwise get an external hard drive. For under a hundred dollars you can get one that will store over a million pictures (a few less if you take a lot of videos).

Or you can use the Cloud. OneDrive is a Microsoft **file hosting service** that allows users to sync files and later access them from a web browser or mobile device. Users can share files publicly or with their contacts; publicly shared files do not require a **Microsoft account** to access them.

Google offers "Google Drive", a file storage and synchronization service. It allows users with a Google account to store files in the cloud, synchronize files across devices, and share them with other people who have a Google account. The first 15 GB's are free.

iCloud is a Cloud storage and Cloud computing service from Apple. The service provides its users with means to store data such as documents, photos, and music on remote servers for download to iOS, Macintosh or Microsoft Windows devices, to share and send data to other users, and to manage their Apple devices if lost or stolen.

Dropbox is yet another up and coming file hosting service.

Remember to calculate the amount of storage that your pictures will take and ensure that the media you are considering has enough room. It is not a good idea to assume that your 16 GB flash drive will hold your entire set of "Trip around the World" photos and videos.

Making multiple backups is usually a good approach. Flash drives and external hard drives have been known to fail. Even though one of my flash drives survived a bout in my washing machine, I don't recommend it. Put your backup pictures in another location if you can (the Cloud is another location). If you are careful and take these precautions, give yourself a pat on the back.

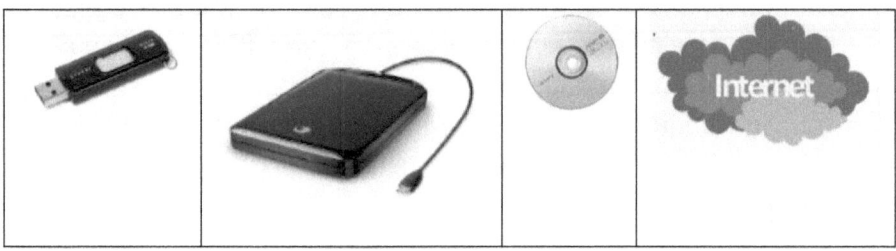

Figure 1 Some backup devices

Bang for the Buck

As you go through the steps in handling your photographs, you have to consider how much time you have. The person with a full-time job and a family may not have a lot of time to spend. On the other hand, a retired person may have a lot of time and the inclination to spend it on managing his / her photographs.

When you are taking pictures while on a vacation, you often have a choice to spend your time looking at the object or taking a good picture of it (I want a picture of the classic car without some tourist standing in front of it. If I have enough time to wait for him to move, I probably could take a professional quality picture. A professional photographer may spend hours or days on one picture. But I usually don't have that kind of time.

The same holds true for organizing and editing your pictures. What do you do? Start with steps that give you a lot of bang for the buck. Later you can fine tune your work. As an example, you can do some editing of your picture so that it looks good for most viewers in most situations. Later, if you have a lot of time, you can do more editing. The first may take minutes and the second hours. If you have enough time and enough inclination (and a little skill) you can get a professional quality picture that only an expert can tell was edited.

Your picture taking device – Some practical ideas

There are numerous devices you can use for taking pictures. The most common is your cell phone. Most people have them, they are small, lightweight and easy to use. However, they have some limitations. They usually are not good with fast motion, low light conditions, and

Photo Phinishing

situations where the object is far away (note: every year, cell phones and smartphones are getting better. The newer ones even have wide angle and telephoto lenses as well as the standard one). Also, if your battery runs out or you run out of memory space, you are out of luck. Cell phones use "digital zoom". It basically takes a portion of the picture and enlarges it. You lose quality when you do this. The picture quality may still be acceptable, but not as good as optical zoom. The pictures below show what digital zoom can do to the quality of the image.

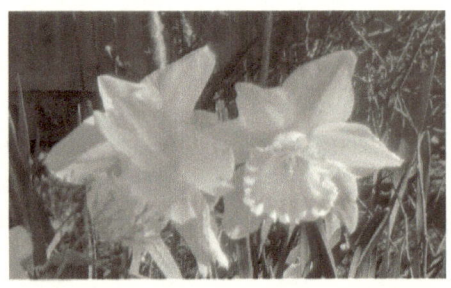

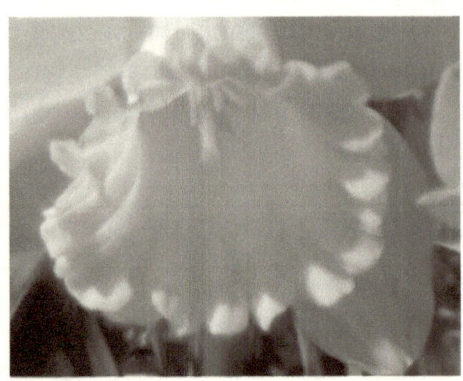

Marc Lipman

If you want better telephoto or wide-angle pictures you can buy auxiliary lenses for your smartphone or buy a smartphone that has multiple lenses.

Digital cameras range from glorified cell phones to professional digital SLR's (with prices to match). You can pick one that meets your needs and budget. Even within a given price range, they are all not the same. Shop carefully. Carrying around an extra battery and an extra SD card is a good idea. A 30 second video may use about 75 MB – as much as 50 hi-resolution pictures. When I was descending Bright Angel Trail in the Grand Canyon (1 hour to get part way down, 2 hours to get back up) I was glad I had an extra battery. Also, my camera had a curious attribute of becoming twice as heavy on the way back up.

Some criteria for judging cameras (Based on your use)

- Price: Prices range from well under a hundred to well over a thousand.

- Pixels: The more pixels, the more you can blow up a picture without having it degrade (be cautious, a lot of megapixels is no substitute for a good lens).

- Quality of the lens: Lens quality varies among cameras. Digital SLR's allow you to buy lenses that better meet your needs. Wide-angle zoom lenses and telephoto zoom lenses let you take pictures of subjects that you could not take with an inexpensive camera (such as a hummingbird in the distance).

- Size and weight of camera: Digital SLR's have more features but are bulkier and heavier.

Photo Phinishing

- Battery life: Unless you want to carry around extra batteries, you should know about how long a charge will last (and whether it takes standard ones like AAA's or ones specific to your camera).

- Response time: Some cameras take a number of seconds between the time they are turned on and the time they are ready to shoot. Some take a number of seconds between the time they shoot a picture and the time they are ready to shoot again. You may lose the chance to take the picture you want (especially with children or grandchildren).

- Features: There are a lot of camera features that may affect your buying decision. They are too numerous to enumerate here (especially since I am NOT an expert in cameras).

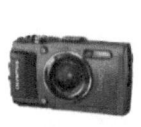 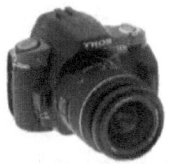

Some people use iPads. One advantage of them is a larger screen so that you can see your pictures better after you take them. Of course, they are bulkier to carry around than a cell phone. You can even get wide angle and telephoto lenses for your iPad.

Marc Lipman

Some notes on color

Color can be a subjective attribute. Sometimes people may want to change the color of a picture, even if the original matches the object. Another factor to consider is that the color you see on your screen is not the same as the one you see on the printer. Changing your monitor settings (you're out of luck if you are using a laptop or tablet) may help and calibration kits can be purchased to reduce the discrepancy. The color on your TV will even look different.

Photo Phinishing

Organizing your pictures

A useful approach when taking pictures is to take a lot of them. If you don't do this and an important one is out of focus, or somebody's head got in the way – tough luck. In the old days of film cameras (those cameras that used sheets of plastic to record pictures), you had to pay money to get all those rolls developed and printed. But now with a digital camera with a 64 GB SD card, you would have a hard time filling it up. Even if you have a cell phone, you should have no trouble if you remember to erase unneeded pictures and videos before you go on a long trip.

When you get back and realize that you should do something with all those pictures, the first step is to look at them and erase the ones that are out of focus, too dark, too light, or a picture of your foot. There are others that you may not be sure of. I always copy them to my PC first just in case I deleted one by accident or one that I may want later. You may have to combine pictures from different sources. On a trip you may have those taken with your digital camera, your wife's iPad and your son's Smartphone. I start by copying them all to my PC.

Another useful technique is to cheat a little. Occasionally you didn't get a picture that you really wanted in order to tell your story. For example, I took a lot of pictures at the botanical garden but forgot to take one of the entrance sign. I may be able to get one from one of my fellow travelers. Or if that fails, I can go to the Internet. Don't forget that sometimes a picture you want is only available in hard copy. Use a scanner! This works well especially when you are making family albums.

> *By The Way: Sometimes a picture fits in more than one folder. For example, a picture of your son and his daughter might go in the "son" folder AND the "granddaughter" folder. Do you copy the picture (and use twice the storage and have the chance of changing one but not the other). Use the Windows "Create Shortcut" feature. That way, there is only one picture file, but it appears in more than one folder. Be careful, shortcuts do NOT appear in slideshows*

Now, where do you put them? This is a personal decision. If you have 50 pictures in your photo collection, putting them in one folder will do. If you have 5,000 pictures, different techniques are required. You have to decide a good way to organize them. Pictures from a trip can be put in their own folder. If the contents of a folder is too big, break it down into subfolders. If you only have a few pictures in each folder, you may want to combine them. Family and Friends pictures can be organized in a similar manner. Remember, this is an ongoing process. As you take more pictures, you may want to reorganize your folders.

For my trip to Australia, I created an "Australia" folder with subfolders for each city I visited. Note: by putting a number as part of the folder name, I can have these folders sorted in the order in which I visited the places.

Photo Phinishing

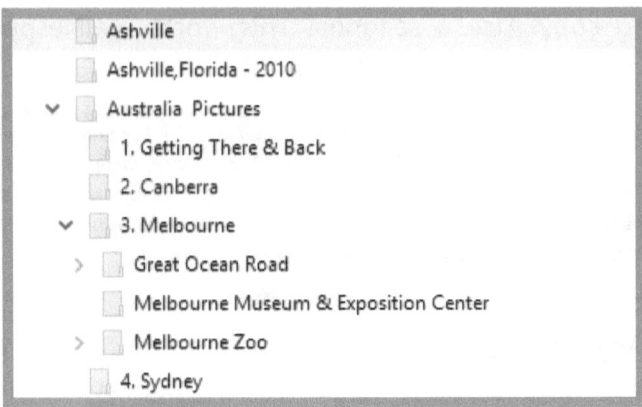

Figure 2 Example of Picture Folders

You may want to rename your picture file names. Somehow "DSC053129.JPG" is not as informative as "Devils Tower.JPG". However, this can become a daunting task if you have taken 300 pictures. Note in the example below I used a two digit prefix to have the pictures appear in the order I desired.

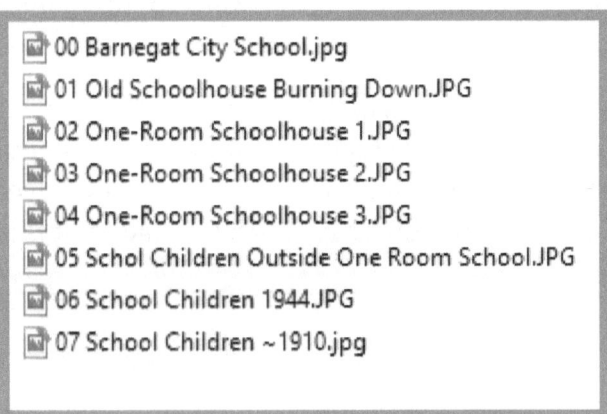

Figure 3 Naming files to display in proper order

Finally, you may still have a lot of pictures that you do not want to throw away but don't want to show in a slideshow. Make an "unused" folder and put them there. That way, they are still available if you need them but are not where they are shown.

Editing your pictures

Editing Concepts

Editing pictures is a topic that could take a whole book in itself. Since I am not an expert in all the editing programs and their techniques, I will only provide a summary of what you can do (with a few examples).

It is important to understand the differences between drawing programs and picture editing programs. Drawing programs work with objects. These objects can be lines, shapes, text, and pictures. The objects can be moved, resized, and deleted. The only thing you can do with a picture is move it or resize it. After you exit from the program, you can go back to it and make more changes, including undoing things you did before (like removing an object).

Picture editing programs work with an image on the screen. You can do many things to the image, such as change its brightness, add text and shapes, or cut and paste pieces from one source to another. However, once you save the changes and exit the program, the changes cannot be undone. Since we are working with photos, we will only talk about picture editors.

There are dozens of programs and Apps that provide editing capabilities. For example, I will pick several:

- Microsoft Paint
- Paint.net
- GIMP
- Pixlr

Marc Lipman

I picked these because they represent: A simple one to use with limited features, one with more features, one with extensive features, and one that runs on multi platforms. Microsoft Paint and Paint.net are available for Microsoft Windows, and GIMP is available under Microsoft Windows, Mac and Linux. All of these are free.

Smartphones and iPads have a number of Apps to edit pictures. They do not have extensive capabilities like GIMP or Photoshop and editing is harder on a small screen but may do well for your needs. Pixlr and PixlrEditor are examples for android and iPad, as well as for PC's and iMacs.

Each of you may have your favorite editor(s) and know all about their features. I am not even going to attempt to list or describe all the apps that are available.

An approach I take when editing a picture is to save the edited one under a different name (ex. "Komodo Dragon Revised.jpg". That way I can go back to the original if I want to. I also can easily tell which ones I have edited (I look for the word "Revised" in the file name).

One of the most common editing tasks is cropping. Often the picture you take has a person or object near an edge that you don't want in the picture: crop it!

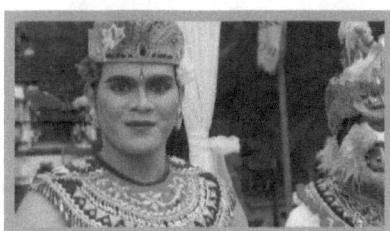 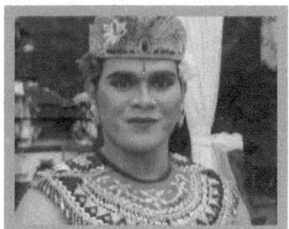

Figure 4 Before and after cropping

Photo Phinishing

Another simple one is adding text to a picture. Sometimes the picture itself is not self-explanatory. Often the object that you knew all about a day after you took the picture is not easy to remember a month afterward. Solution: Add a text box to the picture. And sometimes an object in a picture is not obvious. Add text and a pointer.

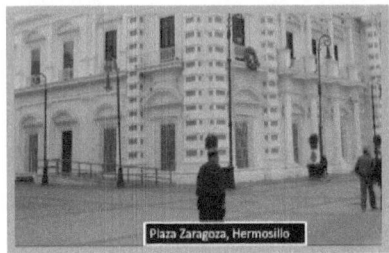 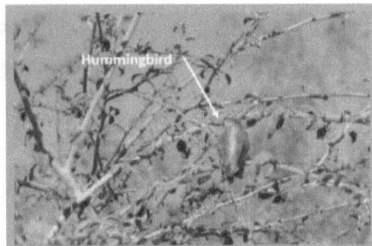

Figure 5 Examples of text boxes and pointers

Adding an inset to a picture may enhance it. Below is a photo of a picture I saw on a cruise ship. The picture was a mosaic of tiny cars. I magnified a close-up of these and added them as an insert.

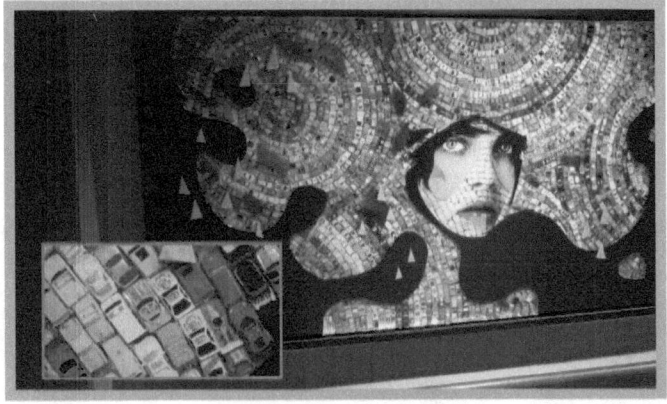

Figure 6 Use of Insets

Something that may involve a little more work is removing an unwanted object(s) from a picture. Often you can use the "copy" and "paste" options in your picture editor. Copy a section from your picture and paste it over the unwanted object. Most editors have a rectangular selection tool; others also have advanced selection tools.

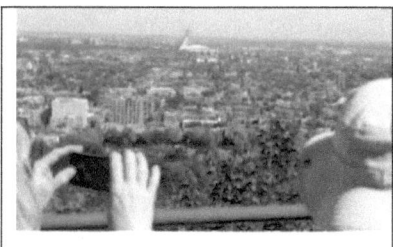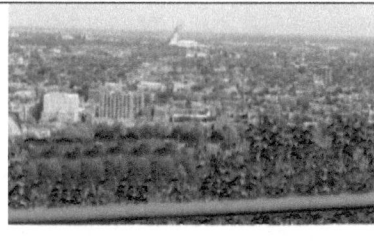

Figure 7 Use of copy and paste

To finish the job, you may have to use the "airbrush" tool to complete the job. You select the color for the airbrush and the type of airbrush and use it to fill in any areas that need it.

Many of the better editors have tools to improve your picture with the click of one button. In Paint.net it is "Adjustments/auto-Level" menu item. In Gimp it is "Colors/Auto/White Balance". Sometimes it works (the new picture is better), sometimes it doesn't.

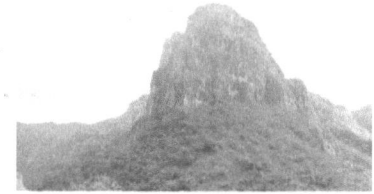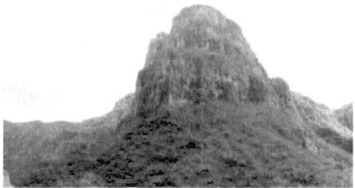

Figure 8 A case where auto correction worked

Photo Phinishing

I liked the second one better and used it.

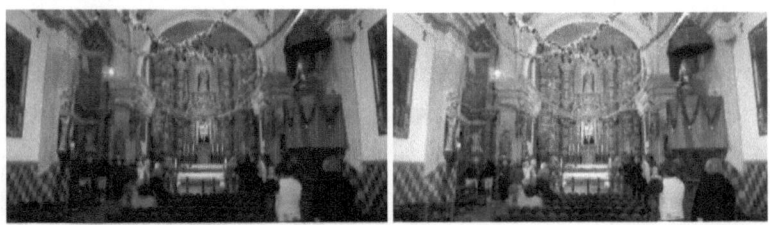

Figure 9 A case where auto correction didn't work

I liked the original one better.

Different photo editors have different features. I pick the editor to use based on what I need.

Features to consider when choosing a Photo Editor(s):

- Cut/Copy/Paste – Copying a piece of a picture and pasting it somewhere else is a very important tool. Rectangular selection is available on PC based editors. Freestyle selection or the ability to choose your area (like a parallelogram) is often desirable and is available on the sophisticated editors.
- Change resolution – If your camera device takes high-resolution pictures, you may want to change the resolution. High-resolution pictures are wonderful if you want to make large sized prints (or even posters). But they use a lot of memory – 2 or 3 MB vs. 300 KB to 1 MB. If you are just displaying them (especially if your device has limited memory), or sending them to others, you may want to use a smaller resolution.

- Cropping – Sometimes a picture may have something on a side, top or bottom that detracts from the picture and should be removed.
- Changing brightness, contrast, or color – The sky's the limit as to what you can do to a picture by altering these. Simple editors let you make these changes to the picture; more sophisticated ones let you change a selected piece of the picture.
- Dodging and burning in – these are techniques derived from the old days of film printing. The photographer could brighten or darken parts of a photograph. This capability is not available in simple editors.
- Special effects – The sky's the limit here too. Different editors have different special effects.

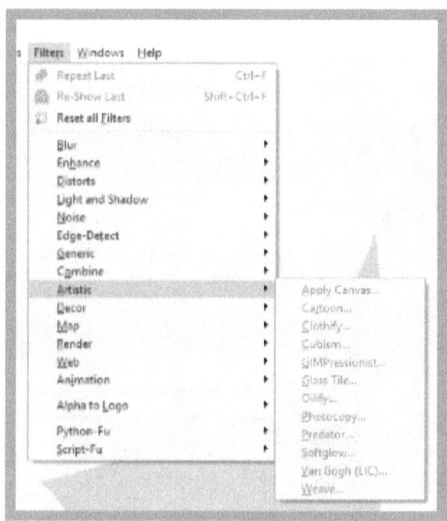

Figure 10 Some Special Effects

Photo Phinishing

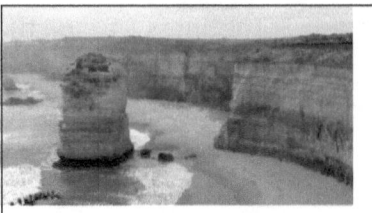

Figure 11 Original picture

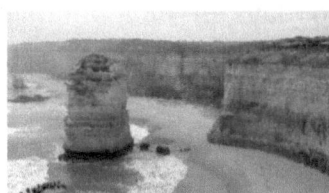 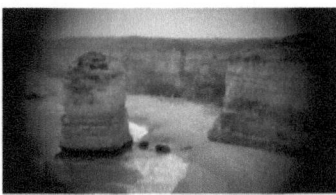

Figure 12   Special effects – Sepia and Vignette

- Painting tools – Tools like a pencil, a paintbrush and an <u>airbrush</u> are available. A color picker lets you pick a color from a spot on your picture to put on your tool, where you can later use it on your pencil or paintbrush.

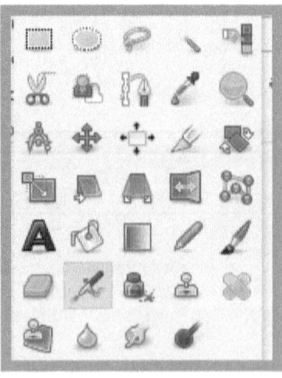

Figure 13 Painting Tools

- GIF files – GIF files are picture files with layers. You can specify the time for each layer to be displayed. Windows picture viewers and PowerPoint slides support GIF files. That means that as the viewer looks at the picture, it changes. Only the more sophisticated editors support GIF files.[1]

As I describe some of these techniques, you may ask yourself, "This sounds good, but I don't know how to do that." Go to **on-line help!** If the program does not have a help menu item or a help button, use Google (or your favorite search engine). You can almost always find an answer and often step-by-step instructions.

FEATURES

FEATURE	Paint	Paint.net	Gimp	Pixr
Rectangular Select	✔	✔	✔	
Enhanced Selection tools		✔	✔	
Cut/Copy/Paste	✔	✔	✔	
Crop	✔	✔	✔	✔
Flip/Rotate	✔	✔	✔	✔
Effects	0	35	> 100	> 50
Color Picker	✔	✔	✔	
Pencil	✔	✔	✔	✔
Paintbrush	✔	✔	✔	
Airbrush			✔	
Layered pictures			✔	
Adjust brightness/Contrast/ …		✔	✔	✔
Inserting text	✔	✔	✔	✔

---

[1] WEB browsers and PowerPoint presentations support GIF files

Photo Phinishing

Repairing / Fixing a Photograph.[2]

Sometimes a photograph you have may be damaged (faded, torn, water-spotted, etc.). If you can scan it into your computer without damaging it any further, you can use your photo editor to repair it. Depending on the damage, the work may be easy or may take hours. Once you have repaired it, you can then print the repaired image on a good photo printer or have it printed online or at a store with printing facilities.

---

[2] If it is a valuable photograph and it involves doing anything to it, leave it to the professionals.

Sharing your pictures

In today's world where most of us bring a camera (a Smartphone is a camera) with us, sharing photos is often desirable. Many of us "E-Mail" photos to friends or relatives (are some people relatives but not friends?). This usually works for small numbers of pictures but may be limited by the size of uploads that your E-Mail system allows (one of mine only allows 20 MB).

When you E-Mail a picture from an iPhone or iPad, select the appropriate file size. A small one will upload and download faster but produce a lower quality picture.

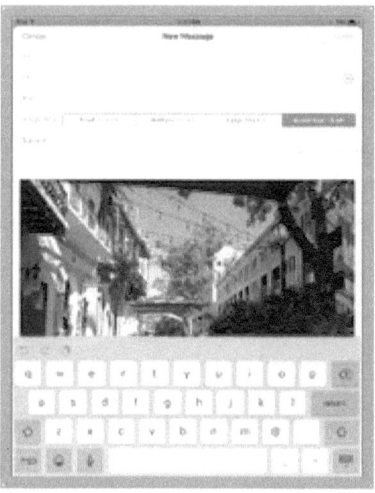

Figure 14 E-Mailing a picture from an iPad

The figures below show the picture sent at two different resolutions, then blown up.

Photo Phinishing

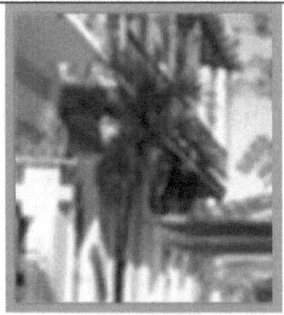
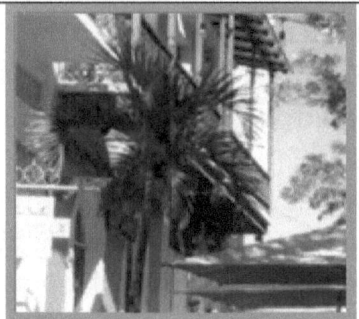

Figure 15 Low Resolution

Figure 16 High Resolution

Using the WEB is good, as long as the two parties have access to it. I use Google Drive to share pictures with others.

If I am visiting someone who may have some photos that I want, I make sure to bring along a flash drive. I make sure that there is enough free space on it (it is embarrassing to have 10 MB of space left on it and 20 MB worth of photos to load).

Social media provides a very popular way to share pictures, with Facebook certainly deserving mention. One of the most popular applications on Facebook is the Photos application, where users can upload albums of photos, tag friends helped by facial recognition technology, and comment on photos. Well over 50 billion user photos have been uploaded to Facebook.

A topic that could have fit under "Sharing your pictures" or "Displaying your pictures" is: "Greeting / Holiday cards." For those who want a personalized one and can't find one after searching through racks of cards, there is a solution. Start with an appropriate picture you have taken. Then create your card. There are internet sites where you can create your own card and send it electronically to your friends and relatives or print it and use "snail mail".

Photo Phinishing

Displaying your pictures

Once you have taken your pictures, organized them, and edited them, you have to decide how to show them. First, you must consider your audience. Aunt Helen will look at dozens of photographs of your two-year-old grandson, but she doesn't like using those newfangled gadgets. Your co-workers don't have the time (or the interest) to look at 70 pictures of the Montreal Botanical Garden. My friend from the Garden Club only wants to see the Montreal Botanical Garden . What do I do?

I try to handle all situations. My phone and iPad will usually have a folder with a "normal" set of pictures as well as one with only the "highlights". That way I can accommodate each audience. If I have a masochistic audience, I also have a PowerPoint presentation with all the pictures AND details about the trip (one of my friends was planning to go to the National Parks and actually wanted to see my presentation).

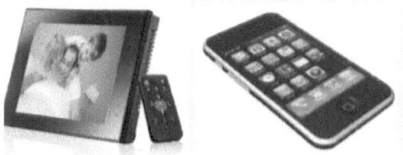

Hardcopy

In the old days (the 70's) you had only a few options for displaying pictures. If you were at home, you would dust off your photo albums and gather your audience around the table. Slide projectors - devices that showed your pictures on a screen in a darkened room - were sometimes used (the bulb would usually burn out in the middle of your show). If you were away from home, you would pull out a few crumpled photographs from your wallet or purse and pass them around.

Hardcopy is still desirable for some situations. You can print your pictures with a standard printer (ink jet or laser) or a photo printer (a printer that is designed for picture printing as well as printing documents). Photo printers use ink that is resistant to deterioration over time and work well with a variety of photo papers. They also have extra features such as being able to preview your pictures on the printer and printing your pictures directly from your storage device or camera. They range in price from ones that are slightly more expensive than standard printers to those that produce professional quality pictures at a much higher price (dye sublimation printers). Printers for home use are limited to the size of the picture that you can print-8 ½ X 11 (unless you spend a **LOT** of money). I usually only use my photo printer when I need a picture printed "FAST". The subject of printers is beyond the scope of this book.

> By The Way: If you are printing something like a party invitation with a picture in it any printer will do.

You can also get your pictures printed online or at a number of stores (my favorite approach). Prices are usually reasonable, often cheaper than it would cost you to print them yourself. You can even get your albums created for you. The service I use will print pictures from 4 X 6 to 20 X 30.

Photo Phinishing

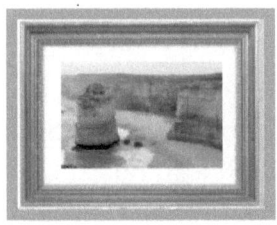

Also, there a lot of other possibilities. One of my favorites is to get a calendar. I choose the option that lets me put in my own events (such as birthdays) on the calendar pages. Of course, each month's picture will be one from my latest excursion. I also got a mug with one the pictures I took on it.

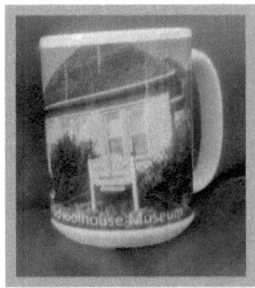

I have not yet used some of the other choices for printing a picture, such as a tee shirt or a birthday cake.

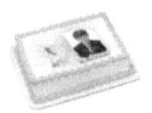 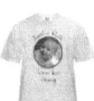 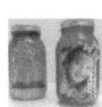 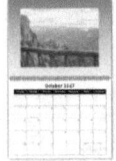 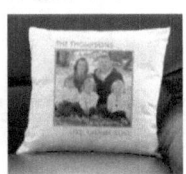

Some factors to consider when buying a photo printer:
- Price
- Cost of cartridges (per picture)
- Picture quality
- Speed

- Reliability
- Features

> **Never** use inkjet photo paper in a laser printer. It will melt into the innards of your printer!!!

Computers

Computers are a desirable way to show pictures since they all have a "Slideshow" feature. With this you can go back and forth to show your pictures. Laptops are portable and be taken almost anywhere. Almost all laptops have HDMI connections, meaning that you can connect them to most modern TV's.[3]

Computers can also display PowerPoint presentations (see the chapter on Presentations).

Cables, Connectors, Adapters and Gadgets

Although most people are reasonably familiar with their device, such as their smart phone or their iPad, they don't always know what cables, connectors and adapters may be useful. They know that a HDMI cable is important. But you can't always get your device close to the TV. What do you do? You can buy a small HDMI male-to-male adapter. Now you can connect two short HDMI cables together to make a long one.

You can buy adapters to connect HDMI cables to your smart phone. Since you can give slideshows on your smart phone (and even show PowerPoint presentations), you can now show them on your TV.

---

[3] I am always cautious as a reader might have a 10 year old computer and a 15 year old TV.

Photo Phinishing

Two things that can happen to your smart phone when taking a lot of pictures and videos are: running out of battery and running out of storage. Both have solutions. You can buy portable batteries that can recharge your smart phone (not instantaneously) and On-The-Go (OTG) cables that let you connect your smart phone to a flash drive.

Suppose you want to show your pictures that are on a SD Card on your TV, but your TV only has a USB connection. Don't worry. You can get a SD to USB adapter. You plug your SD Card into the adapter and plug it into your USB connection on your TV. If you have a Mini SD or Micro SD, they come with an SD adapter.

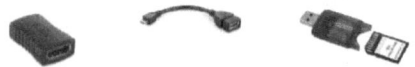

Figure 17 some connection devices

I couldn't resist the urge to add a few words about some "gadgets". When I talk about bringing my PC to a friend's house to show them some pictures, you would guess properly that I am referring to my laptop. Even I am not masochistic enough to bundle up my system unit, monitor, keyboard and mouse and bring them there. However I (since I am into gadgets) might bring one of my special desktop units, my "Raspberry Pi". This PC is about the size of a deck of cards. You plug it into your TV with a HDMI cable, attach a power transformer (like the one you use to charge your smart phone), connect the mouse and keyboard of your choosing, and you are ready. I also have a C.H.I.P. computer. It is half the size and half the cost of the Raspberry Pi. It does not have all the features of the Raspberry Pi, but it will show pictures.

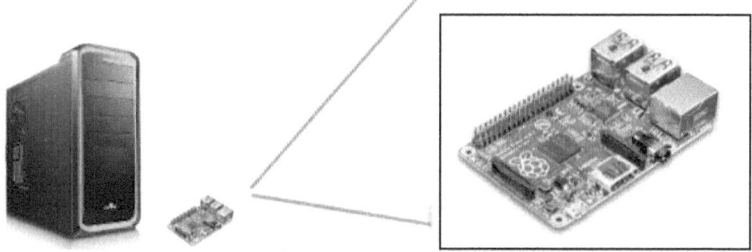

Figure 18 Relative size of a PC and a Raspberry Pi

More about Viewers & Slideshows

Viewers are available on PCs and other devices. Most viewers have features to enhance your viewing. Of course, they let you advance to the next picture or go back to the previous one. They also let you zoom in (or zoom out) on a picture, rotate a picture (occasionally you forget to do this when editing the pictures) and edit the picture.

Photo Phinishing

The slideshow feature (auto-advance) helps, especially when you are in a situation where you are not there to control the show. I was at a birthday party at a catering hall. I had made a presentation for (of) the guest of honor. With a small flat screen TV and a laptop, I was able to show the slides (pictures) without controlling them. Of course, PowerPoint slideshows can be run manually or automatically. If you have organized your folders properly and named your files properly, your slideshow should flow smoothly.

When (and if) you read the section on "Presentations" you may ask yourself, "why go to all that work when I can create picture files with text, insets and pointers on them?" There is a reason. Sure, you can do all those things to a picture file using a photo editor. If you do something wrong, you can even undo it. But once the file is saved and the photo editor program closed, that's it! You can't undo your changes. You have to change it again. It's like touching up a painting. Once the paint dries, that's it.

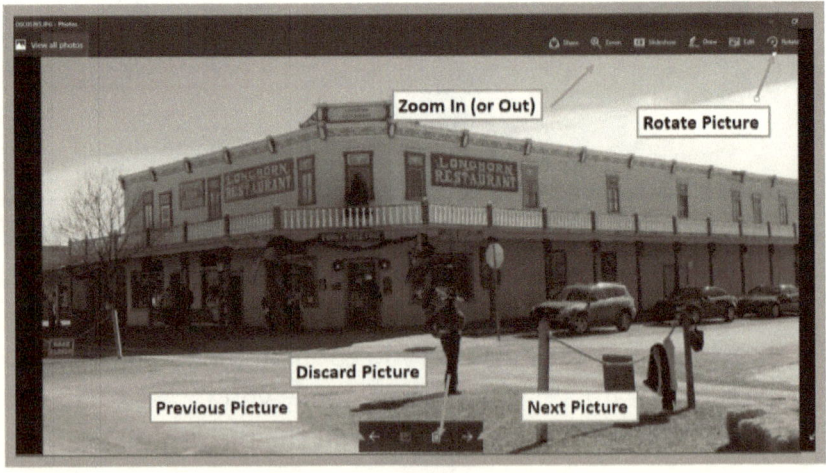

Figure 19 The Microsoft Windows viewer

Your Smartphone, your iPad, your Kindle, your Digital Picture Frame

With a Smartphone you have several ways to view your pictures. Android Smartphones have folders similar to those on your PC. Apps like "Gallery" and "Photos" let you view your pictures in a variety of ways.

The "Photos" app on the iPad lets you organize your pictures by albums. It has a slideshow feature and some picture editing facilities.

Digital picture frames are another way to display your pictures. They can be placed on a bookcase, shelf or table for viewing by all. Typical frame size is about 10 inches, but smaller and larger ones are available. The traditional way to transfer your digital pictures to a digit picture frame was to use a flash drive. Several brands even allow friends or family members to E-Mail their pictures directly to your picture frame using the internet (they have to have permission). No work is required on the part of the person receiving the picture.

Your Camera

Obviously, the main purpose of your camera is to take pictures. Looking at the pictures you took through the camera's viewfinder or its 3-inch screen leaves a lot to be desired. However, many cameras have a mini HDMI connector and the cable to connect it to your TV. Thus, you can do slideshows with it. This is desirable when you would like to show your pictures before you have had time to copy them to your PC and organize them.

TVs

TVs are a wonderful way to share your pictures with a small number of people. As mentioned before, you can connect your PC or any portable device with an HDMI connection to your TV. In addition, most current TVs have a connection for a SD card or a flash drive (or both). An APP on the TV lets you have a slideshow without having to connect another device to it.

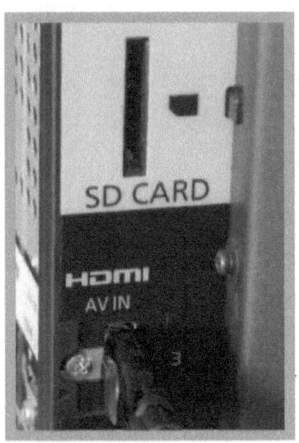

Figure 20 Example of a TV's SD CARD Slot

Projectors

If you want to show your pictures to a larger audience, a projector may be for you. They are available at many electronics stores for under $500 (note: sometimes a replacement bulb may be almost as expensive as the original unit.) The more inexpensive ones may have a lower intensity bulb and may require a darker room. They can be fastened to any computer or device that has an HDMI connector. I even have a HDMI cable for one of my Smartphones.

On the Internet

There are several ways to view your pictures on the Internet. One way is to have a website. You can put your pictures there and anyone with access to the WEB can view them. Of course, you have to purchase a website (they're inexpensive) and learn how to create the site (it's easy).

Google Drive allows users with a Google account to store files in the cloud, synchronize files across devices, and share them with other people who have a Google account.

Video

Video often makes a desirable supplement to your pictures. In the old days, special cameras were required to take video. Now virtually all Smartphones, tablets, iPads and digital cameras can take quality video. Some of the ways of working with pictures are the same as those for video, some are different, and some don't apply at all.

It is just as important to back up your videos as it is to back up your pictures. Remember most videos take up a lot more space than pictures.

Video files can be organized the same way as picture files. Sometimes you may want to keep them in a separate folder.

Editing video files require separate tools. The picture editing programs previously mentioned do NOT work with video files. There are a few free video file editors that can do simple editing like cutting and pasting sections of a video (the equivalent of using a scissors and tape to edit 8 MM movies).

One app that runs on android and iPad lets you rotate your footage, change its aspect ratio or choose a template theme you like.

Professional quality programs (with prices to match) can do almost anything and are available for Windows and iMac. They often require a fast PC with a lot of RAM and a good graphics card.

Video files can be displayed on PC's, Smartphones, TV's and tablets.

Your slideshow program will usually play video, and video can be included in your PowerPoint presentations. Caution: Adding a 30-minute video of your granddaughter's belly-dancing performance to your slideshow is usually not a good idea.

Obviously, hardcopy or putting a video on an E-Book doesn't apply (you can take a snapshot of a video frame and use it.

Presentations

Presentations deserve their own section. PowerPoint, and its free cousin – Impress, give you features that ordinary slideshows can't. Of course, this comes with a price. First, you have to have one of these programs on your PC or portable device. You can buy PowerPoint for your PC, Mac, or your Smartphone. LibreOffice can be downloaded for free to your Windows PC, your Linux PC, or your Mac.

Then you have to learn how to use them. I will not describe the basics of how to use PowerPoint here since a number of textbooks and introductory computer courses are available. The features that I describe are also available in LibreOffice Impress unless noted.

I will describe the features and techniques specifically involved in handling your pictures and developing presentations that actually captivate your audience. First, they allow you to easily add textual information to your presentation.

DAY 6, Sunday - Train to Copper Canyon

- Breakfast at hotel and on bus to train station by 7:30
- Took the Chihuahua al Pacifico railroad (Chepe) to the Copper Canyon
  - 132 mile trip – 6 hours (bus took 18 hours)
  - Lunch on the train
  - Arrived at the Hotel Mirador at about 2:30 in the afternoon
  - A welcoming drink, then off to inspect our room
  - Introduction to the Tarahumara Indian culture
  - Dinner & talking with fellow travelers

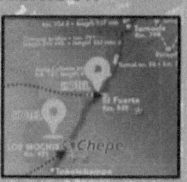

Figure 21 Example of a PowerPoint slide

A trick I use is to create a slide for the day's activities as soon as possible (somehow little details and names seem to get lost if you don't document them). I can always add the picture slides later. This slide can have a background picture. Use one of yours. But usually the colors of the picture interfere with the viewer's ability to read the text. What do you do? Fade the background image. I found that a 50% fade usually does the trick (I did this in the above figure).

PowerPoint has a feature that lets you create a slideshow from the list of pictures that you specify. If you specify a folder with 200 pictures, PowerPoint will make a new presentation with 200 slides (note: LibreOffice Impress doesn't have this feature). Once you have the presentation, you can easily rearrange the slides. This is wonderful since you don't always take pictures in the order that you would like to show them. Rearranging computer files in a folder (by renaming them) is a real pain.

The images you have imported are the resolution (size) of the original picture. This may make the presentation file BIG. This is OK if you have plenty of room on your device and don't have to upload / download it with a slow internet connection (or if you are running out of bandwidth). PowerPoint has a "compression" option. It will resize your image (or all of them) to a smaller resolution. I used this approach for my presentations. In one case, the standard one took 52MB, the compressed one, 10 MB. I keep both copies on my external hard drive.

You can put multiple pictures on a slide (as shown above) as well as text, shapes and list boxes. You can also put audio and video on a slide. I downloaded a Mexican folk song, put it on the opening slide and set it to play automatically and stop when the viewer went to the next slide. Any of these objects can be altered or removed at any time (You can make changes to a picture with a photo editor but cannot undo them after you exit from the program).

Hyperlinks to other slides, presentations or a website can add to your presentation. For example, in your slide about Devils Tower, you can put in a link to the National Parks website about it (remember, you will need an internet connection to get there).

A useful PC program is the "Snipping Tool". It uses the computer equivalent of a pair of scissors. You can take a part of anything that is on your screen (a picture,

44

something from the internet, or some text), snip it and then paste it onto a slide. Once it is there you can resize it or move it as needed.

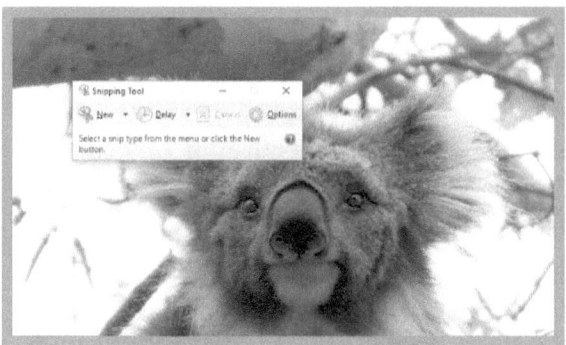

Figure 22 The Snipping Tool

.GIF files sometimes have a place. Remember, they are picture files containing one or more layers. Each layer can be displayed for a period of time (specified when you create or edit the file). A .GIF file placed on your introductory slide may entertain your viewers while you are getting ready to start your presentation.

Another feature that makes your presentations more versatile is the ability to create "Custom Slideshows". This means that the same presentation file may have a "Highlights", a "Normal" and a "Detailed" presentation. You can choose which one to present based on your audience.

Suppose you have created a beautiful slideshow, but don't have a way to show it (your friends in Germany have a TV that accepts a SD card and shows the pictures on it, but they don't have PowerPoint). You can save your presentation as picture files (.JPGs). PowerPoint will let you save the entire presentation as a set of picture files in a folder that you name. This also works if you have to display them on a PC that doesn't have PowerPoint or Impress.

If they have a PC running Microsoft Windows, but don't have PowerPoint, you have another solution. You can save your presentation as an executable (a program file that will run by itself). When they open the file, the slideshow starts running. Of course, they can't edit it or look at how it was made, but so what.

Some hints when preparing a presentation (things your PowerPoint tutorial won't tell you):

- Make it the right length
- Make it informative
- Don't make the slides too busy
- Don't get carried away with colors and effects
- Consider your audience(s)

Finally, entertain your viewers!!!

Why do I need a PC anyway?

As you read this you may ask yourself, "Why do I need a PC to work with my pictures? I have smart devices."

Maybe you don't need one. Apps on my smartphone and my iPad let me delete, rotate, and crop my pictures after I take them. I can also add special effects. I can create albums. And new apps are becoming available all the time.

But sometimes I want more. My smart devices do not have editing tools such as "airbrush" and enhanced copy/paste tools. You may want these features. How about adding text and shapes?

A situation I had involved a picture of the dinner menu for a cruise I was on. The picture was just barely readable

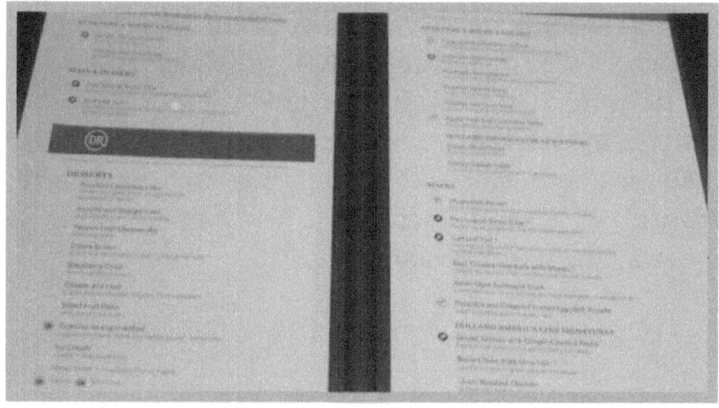

Figure 23 Unreadable text

Does the following look better?

Photo Phinishing

A Typical Menu

Mains

Mushroom Ravioli
Garlic cream sauce, forest mushrooms, tomato concasse
Pan-seared Arctic Char
Parsnip puree, arugula oil, roasted Italian vegetables
Surf and Turf
Filet Mignon, lobster tail, herb garlic butter, porcini basmati rice
Basil Crusted Veal Rack with Morels
Loaded mashed potatoes, zucchini peals, Brussel sprouts
Asian-Style Rotisserie Duck
Sweet-and-Sour sauce, sesame stir-fried vegetables, fried egg noodles
Pistachio and Cheese-Crusted Eggplant Piccata
Israeli couscous, garlic tomato ragu

Figure 24 Readable

Not easy to do with your smart device!

Here's another one. Have you ever taken a picture of a number of people (maybe even distant family members) and later forgot who some of them were? This is something I did! It had to do with a school event of the 40's. I scanned in the picture, faded it out, added the numbers, and passed it out to the people who were there. A few of them were able to remember most of the students. I then typed in the names after the corresponding number, voila!

Marc Lipman

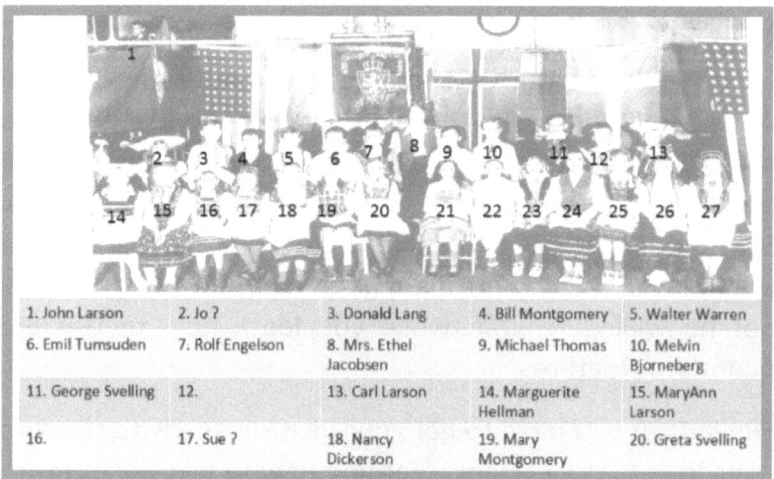

1. John Larson	2. Jo ?	3. Donald Lang	4. Bill Montgomery	5. Walter Warren
6. Emil Tumsuden	7. Rolf Engelson	8. Mrs. Ethel Jacobsen	9. Michael Thomas	10. Melvin Bjorneberg
11. George Svelling	12.	13. Carl Larson	14. Marguerite Hellman	15. MaryAnn Larson
16.	17. Sue ?	18. Nancy Dickerson	19. Mary Montgomery	20. Greta Svelling

Figure 25 Example of picture with names

Other PC capabilities are sometimes valuable. PowerPoint has simple ways to arrange your pictures and set up sophisticated slideshows. How many of you have PowerPoint on your smart device (especially a full-featured version)?

Plus, I don't feel comfortable working with a small screen on changes to pictures that I may display on my large flat screen TV.

My digital camera is much better than my smart phone or my iPad for taking pictures under non-standard situations (low light, fast motion, etc.), but it does not have picture editing capabilities. Also, a 2 X 3 inch screen is certainly not a good tool for critiquing pictures.

For those reasons, I feel much more comfortable having a PC for working with my pictures. Decide for yourself!

Practice makes ~~perfect~~ possible

As you read this, you may agree that some of these techniques are new to you and may be useful. If you already know these things, I am preaching to the choir. If not, practice is important. If you get a brand new digital SLR, learning how to use it while you're on a tour of Komodo Island may not be a good idea. The dragons may not be willing to wait while you learn how to use the panoramic feature.

Similarly, if you have to get your pictures ready to show to your friends in Germany, learning how to use the airbrush in a short period of time is futile.

Practicing software techniques is a lot different from practicing hardware techniques – it doesn't cost you anything (other than time). When you practice something involving cutting wood or painting on canvas, your pieces are wasted. If you practice editing pictures, all you have lost is some time. Remember, MAKE A COPY of your file before working on it.

Picture File Formats

File formats are the way that picture information is stored on the camera, smartphone, tablet or PC.

JPEG file format

The most common format for picture files is: JPEG (Joint Photographic Experts Group). JPEGs are compressed files. How does this work? Suppose that you were wearing a bright red sweater outside on a sunny day. Do all parts of the sweater look the same? Where the sun hits it, it is bright red. Where there are shadows, it is darker. There might be a number of shades, each one slightly different. If you represented the colors exactly, that would take a lot of memory. Each pixel requires 3 bytes of storage (for red, green and blue). If your camera has a 10 megapixel sensor, this would be about 30 megabytes of storage for ONE picture. You would soon run out of space on your memory card. But, suppose you said, "these two colors are so close that we will represent them with one color". We'll use a different format for holding the information. That's the concept behind JPGs. The technique is called *lossy compression*. You lose a little quality, but you save a lot of storage. Because it is *lossy compression*, you can never get the original quality back, but so what.

GIF's

GIF (Graphics Interchange Format) use a lossless compression and can have more than one frame in the file. Each frame can contain a separate picture which can be displayed for a specified time. They can be used in PowerPoint and on WEB pages when you want to show more than one picture on a given space. If you use a lot of frames, you can get animation (like the cartoonists did in

Photo Phinishing

the old days by putting similar pictures on paper and showing one after another quickly).

Raw file formats

If you are taking pictures for the cover of a magazine or for a museum, or you want to make a poster, you may want a better format. "Raw", bitmap and TIFF are uncompressed formats. The quality is better, but they require more storage space. As an example, the same picture that uses 3 megabytes of storage for a JPG may use over 20 megabytes of storage for a TIFF.

Other picture file formats

There are a number of other file formats used for pictures. PNG (Portable Networks Graphics) is a format commonly used to store web graphics, digital photographs, and images with transparent backgrounds. This can be useful on PowerPoint or WEB pages where you want to put one picture on top of another. In the example below, I started with a map of Northern Thailand on a PowerPoint slide. I downloaded a bridge icon and deleted the white parts of the picture using Paint.net. I then pasted it on top of the map on the slide. Note that the map background shows through.

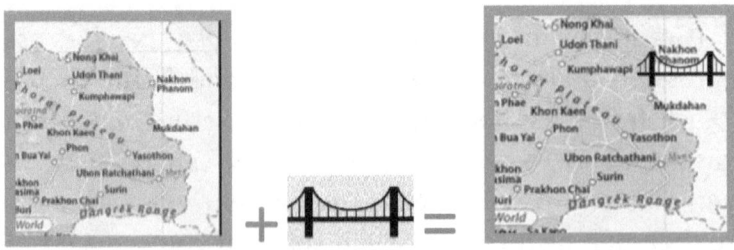

Microsoft Paint and Pant.net use PNG by default.

Video file formats

Video files also can use different file formats. MP4 is a common one for smartphones and digital cameras. MP4 file sizes are relatively small but the quality remains high even after compression. They can be played on many devices.

A 30 second video may take almost 80 megabytes. Compare this to the 3 megabytes for a JPG picture.

Photo Phinishing

Some Definitions

Byte, Kilobyte, Megabyte, Gigabyte, Terabyte: Units of data storage. A byte is the smallest of unit of addressable storage and can hold a character or a piece of a picture, etc.

Kilobyte: 1,000 bytes

Megabyte: 1,000 kilobytes

Gigabyte: 1,000 megabytes

Terabyte: 1,000 gigabytes

Digital SLR: A digital camera where the image from the lens is what you see in the viewfinder or display. Most digital SLRs have interchangeable lenses (wide-angle, telephoto, etc.) so you can pick ones to enhance your picture taking ability. Filters are also available.

Digital zoom: A function of a digital camera or smartphone used to make the image seem more close-up. Digital zoom on a digital camera works the same as cropping and enlarging a photo in a graphics program. When you digitally zoom, you use some quality.

Google Drive: An internet file storage and synchronization service developed by Google. Google Drive allows users to store files in the cloud, synchronize files across devices, and share files.

Hyperlinks: A highlighted word or picture that you can click on to go to another place in the presentation or a different presentation or a Web page.

IOS: A mobile operating system created and developed by Apple Inc. exclusively for its hardware. It is the operating system that presently powers many of the company's mobile devices, including the iPhone, iPad, and iPod Touch.

Linux: A free and open source software Unix-like operating system for computers. Linux is available for most PCs and comes with a number of applications including word processors, photo editing programs and presentation programs. The user can also download an extensive set of applications for their specific needs.

Multimedia: Content that uses a combination of different content forms such as text, audio, images, animations and video.

OneDrive: A file-hosting service operated by Microsoft as part of its suite of online services. It allows users to store files as well as other personal data in the cloud. Files can be synced to a PC and accessed from a web browser or a mobile device, as well as shared publicly or with specific people.

Operating System (O/S): The program that supports a computer's basic functions, such as scheduling tasks, executing applications, and displaying information. Windows, Linux and MAC OS are examples. Ubuntu is a Linux O/S that runs on PC's and is free.

Photo Album: A PowerPoint file created by selecting the "insert new photo album" feature in PowerPoint and selecting the files you want in that album.

Photo Phinishing

Photo Editor: A program / app that allows the user to make changes to a picture file.

Pixel: (a word invented from "picture element") is the basic unit of programmable color on a computer display, printer or digital camera. The more pixels used to represent an image, the closer the result can resemble the original.

PowerPoint: A Microsoft program (part of Microsoft Office) that allows you to create presentations and view them as slideshows (or print them). It was developed for making business presentations but can also be used for personal use. LibreOffice Impress is a free program with most of the features of PowerPoint.

SD Card: A type of memory card typically used in digital cameras and other portable devices. They come in a number of sizes and capacities.

Select Tool: A picture editor tool that lets you select an area of the picture. A tool to select a rectangular or elliptical area is common. Some editors have a free select tool that lets you make an irregular shaped selection.

Social Media: Forms of electronic communication (such as Web sites and Facebook) through which people create online communities to share information, ideas, personal messages, etc.

Video Editor: A program / app that allows the user to make changes to a video file. They range from simple ones that can do things like trim a file to ones that can make your footage look like a Hollywood film.

Marc Lipman

For the Linux Lovers

Linux is a free <u>operating system</u> that runs on a number of computers (PC's, Raspberry Pi's and the C.H.I.P. computer). It can also be run as a virtual machine under Microsoft Windows. Some things are very much alike and some things have differences.

Linux supports Gimp. So, editing pictures can be the same as doing it under Microsoft Windows.

Linux also supports LibreOffice Impress (Its equivalent of PowerPoint). There are some differences here. "Faded background" images will NOT be faded. PowerPoint "Custom Slideshows" will not be available (Impress has its own "Custom Slideshows"). Sometimes text will not be displayed properly due to font differences.

Linux has Slideshow viewers. The GNOME image viewer looks very much like the Microsoft Windows "Raspbian", the Raspberry Pls O/S, has "GPicView". Even the C.H.I.P. computer (the basic computer with a HDMI interface currently sells for about twenty-five dollars) has "Viewnior", a Slideshow viewer with similar features.

Linux does NOT support "Shortcuts". Its equivalent is "Links" They are similar in concept but not compatible with each other.

A real example

Here are the steps I used recently when I made a slideshow of my tour to Copper Canyon in Mexico.

- Every morning I would make a PowerPoint slide of our activities of the previous day.

When I got home I:

- Copied the pictures from my camera, my phone and my wife's phone to my PC.
- I removed the bad ones (out of focus, under or over exposed, and the ones of my foot) and the duplicate (or almost duplicate) ones.
- I created subfolders for each day's pictures (I could tell by the file date when they were taken).
- I took the ones that looked like the auto-fix option in Gimp would correct and tried it. If it worked, I save the file with "Revised" as part of the name. *
- I edited the set of pictures that I took through the windshield of the bus and had an object dangling down and removed it (using Gimp).*
- I created PowerPoint picture albums for each day's pictures.
- I edited each picture album file to put the slides in the order that I wanted. I hid the ones that I probably didn't want (I removed some of them later).
- I added text and arrows to the slides that needed them. *
- I ran it and my wife and I made more corrections after seeing it.

Photo Phinishing

- I created a custom slideshow for each picture album that had a small set of pictures and named it "hilites". *
- I put hyperlinks in the main file so that clicking on that link would bring the viewer to that picture album. *
- I compressed all the pictures in each picture album file and saved the file with "Compressed" in the name. *
- I tested each presentation file on my Raspberry Pi computer running LibreOffice Impress and made a few corrections so that my presentations would run under either PowerPoint or Impress. *
- I saved the "photo album" presentations as picture file folders (each slide was a .jpg file). *

* Not for the beginner

Whew, that was a lot of work!

Anatomy of a slideshow

Here are the details about the final product - the PowerPoint presentation of The Copper Canyon Tour.

- Most of the pictures were taken with a Sony digital SLR, with a few taken with smartphones (carrying a digital SLR with you when traversing a canyon deeper that the Grand Canyon on a zip-line is NOT advisable).
- The main PowerPoint presentation consisted of a title slide, 16 informational slides and 20 picture slides. The title slide played Mexican folk music when the slideshow was started. The music stopped when the next slide is selected.
  - There were 2 custom slideshows – a "hilites" one that showed all the slides and a "full" one that skipped the pictures (they were shown in the photo albums).
  - The informational slides had background pictures, taken from my photographs and faded 50%.
  - The presentation file was 90 megabytes and 26 megabytes when the pictures were compressed.
  - The informational slides had hyperlinks to the associated photo album
- There were 7 photo albums, each one with the pictures about each place we visited.
  - Each photo album had a "regular" custom slideshow with the pictures that most

viewers would like to see. It was the default presentation.

- o Each photo album had a title slide with a background picture.
- o The photo albums had from 29 to 115 slides (25 to 78 in the "regular" custom slideshow.
- o The photo albums ranged in size from 37 megabytes to 1,233 megabytes (6 megabytes to 174 megabytes when compressed).
- The whole presentation had 8 title slides, 321 picture slides (normal view) and used 1.9 gigabytes (430 megabytes compressed) of disk space.

References

Gimp: https://www.gimp.org/

Google Drive: https://www.google.com/drive/

Paint.net: https://ww.getpaint.net/

Ubuntu: https://www.ubuntu.com/

Photo Phinishing

Appendices

Somewhere I read that an appendix is something small, of no apparent use, and can be removed with no adverse effect. Judge for yourself!

Appendix 1: How this e-book was written

The initial concept came from a set of classes that I gave at a public library. The topics started with the ones on the PowerPoint slides for the class and were enhanced.

The pictures used here were taken with a Sony 20-megapixel A58 digital SLR with an 18 to 55 mm zoom lens.

The e-book was written in Microsoft Word and saved in ".HTML" format. Microsoft Notepad was then used to edit the level one and level two headings to create the Table of Contents in e-book format. "Mobipocket Creator" was then used to create the e-book in ".prc" format. Calibre was then used to convert the file from ".prc" format to 'mobi" format.

Appendix 2: Fixing a picture with GIMP

Sometimes a picture you have taken is good, except for an object (or person) that you don't want there. Sometimes the effort in removing it (or him / her) is too complicated or almost impossible, but often a little effort can result in a noticeably better picture. Following are the detailed steps that can be used to do this.

Sometimes the area to be replaced is rectangular, but often the area is more complicated. The editor I am using is GIMP since it has the needed tools (like a "free select" tool). GIMP is free and runs on a number of computer

Photo Phinishing

platforms. Let's assume that we have GIMP running on our PC.

- Run GIMP and open the picture file you wish to fix using "Open" under the "File" menu.

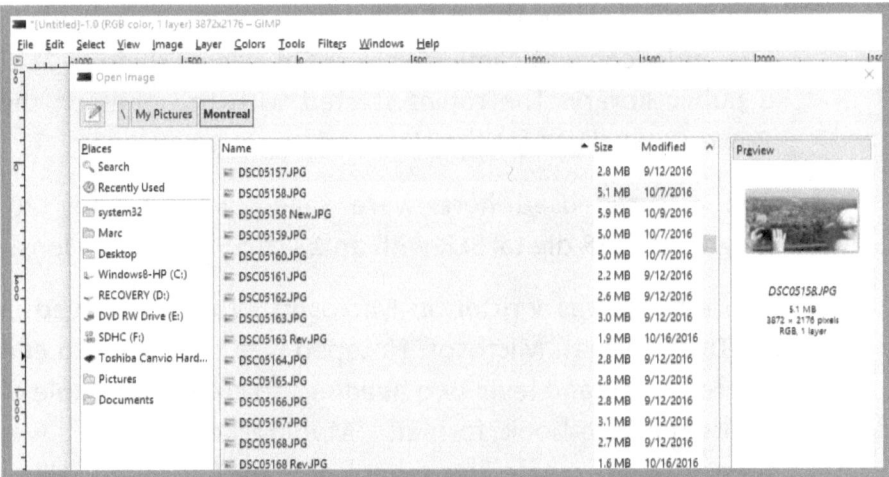

- When the file is opened it should look like this:

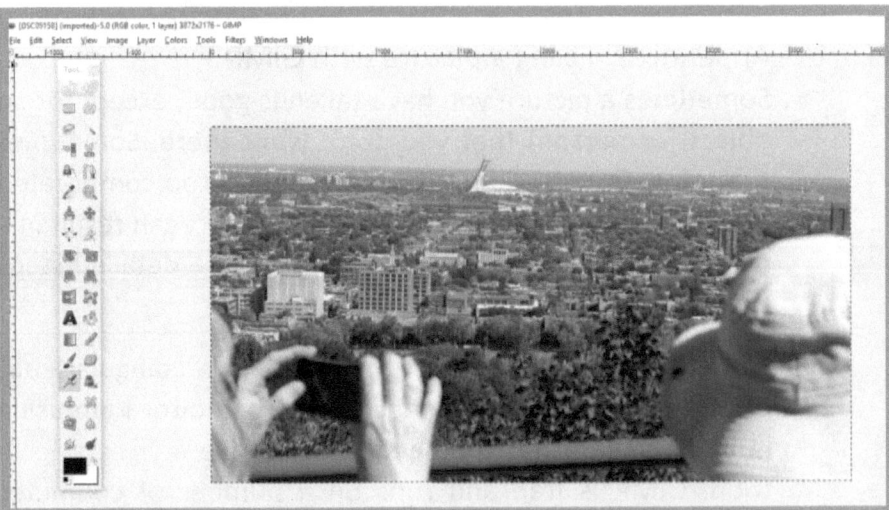

Marc Lipman

You really don't want the hands and the hat in the picture! Let's copy a piece of the picture that we want to replace the hands with.

- Use the free-form select tool to select a piece of the picture. Click on the first spot, move the mouse to the next spot, etc. The last spot should be the point where you started (note that the selection is not a rectangle).

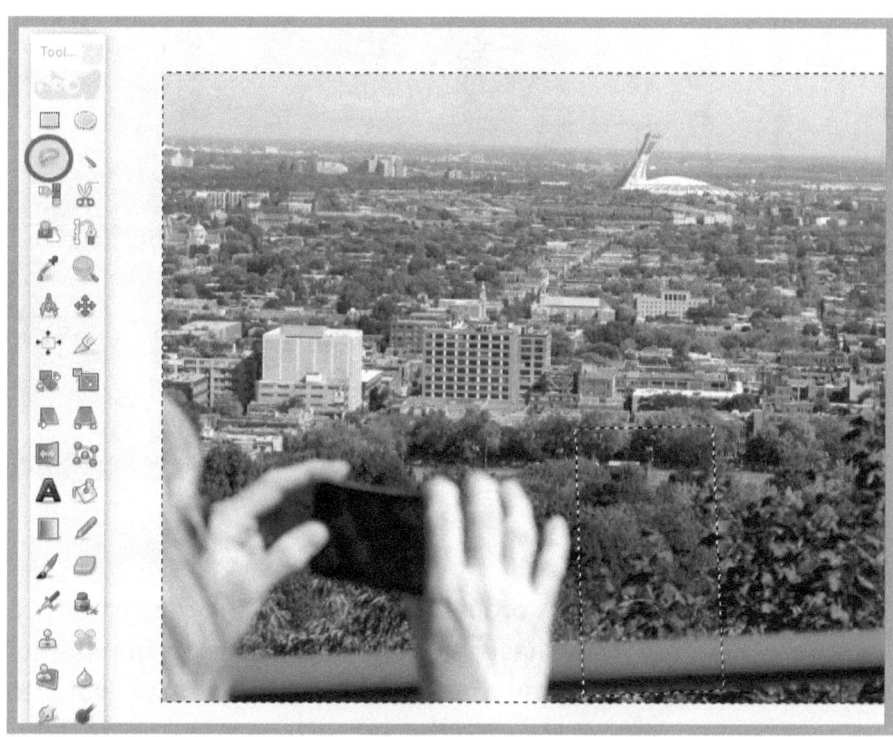

- Now in the "Edit" menu, press "Copy", then "Paste". Move the mouse pointer to the selected piece, press and hold the left button, move the piece to the place you want and release the button.

Photo Phinishing

If the piece is not where you want it, press "Undo" in the "Edit" menu. The result should look like this:

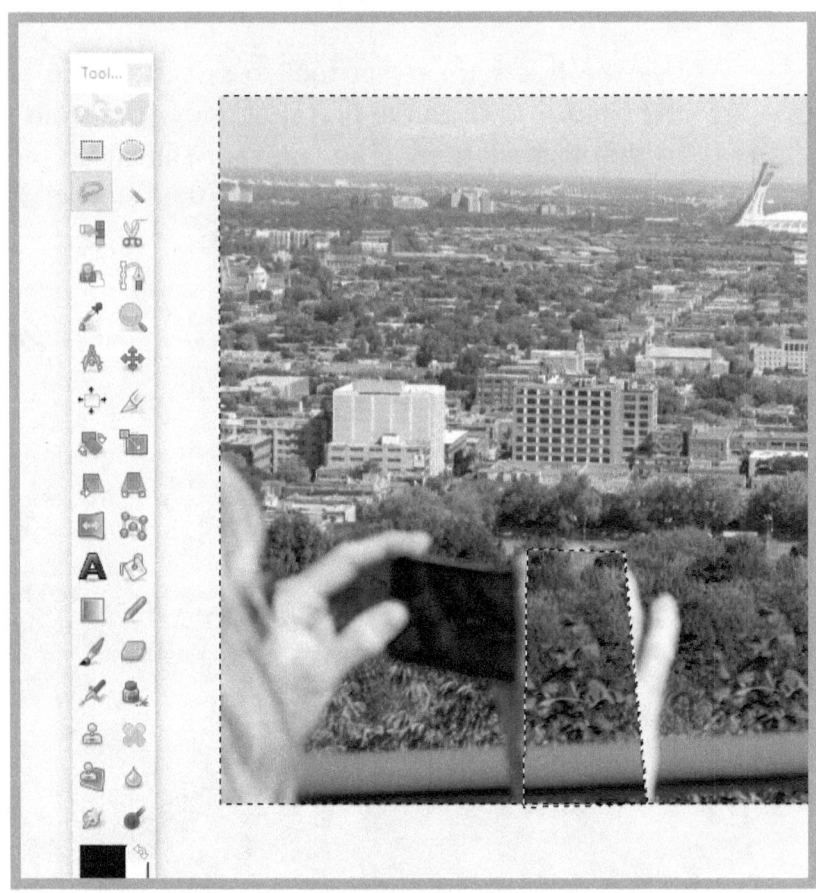

- Repeat this process until you get the desired effect. You may have to copy and paste a number of pieces to do this. Sometimes you may want to finish up by using the airbrush on a few areas. After you are done, the product may look like this:

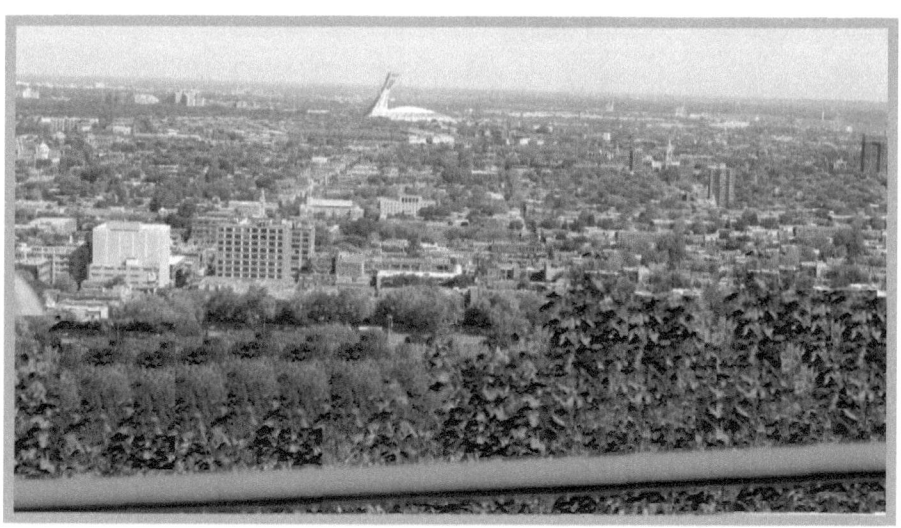

Appendix 3: Using the Airbrush

Sometimes correcting a picture involves more than just copying and pasting. Sometimes the piece you just pasted in does not quite fit. This is an enlargement of a small piece of a picture.

Photo Phinishing

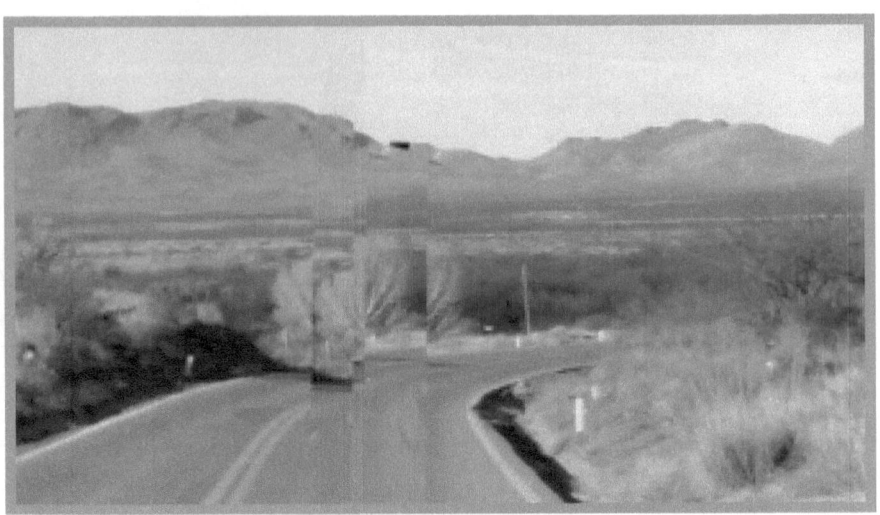

- First use the color picker tool to select the color you want for your airbrush by selecting it and clicking on the spot on the picture containing the color.
- Then select the airbrush tool.

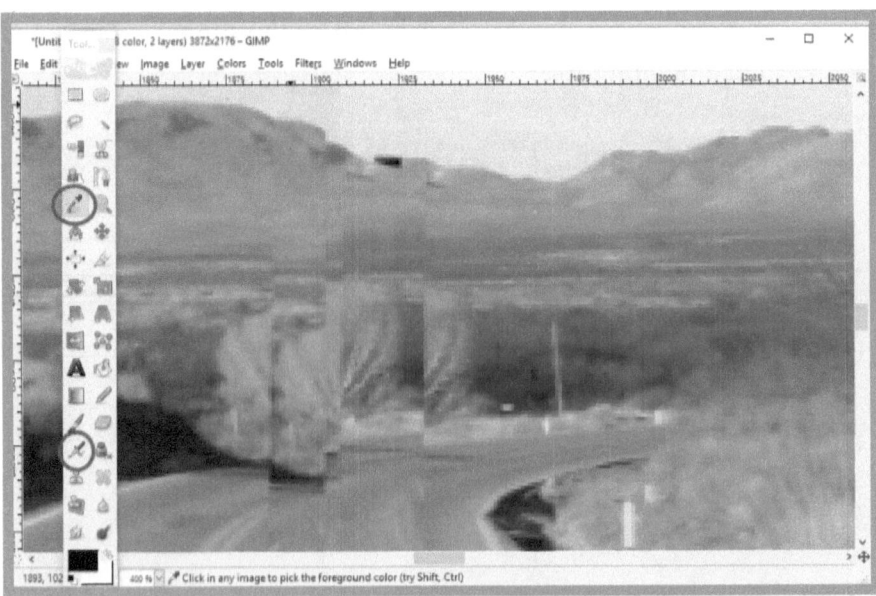

- You can select the type and size of the airbrush - make sure you have set the option in GIMP to show these as indicated below (Under the Edit menu select Preferences, then Toolbox and make sure the "Show active brush, pattern & gradient is checked).

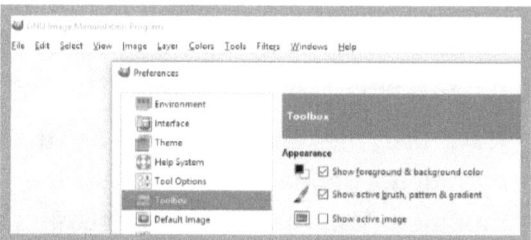

If this option is setup you can change the airbrush if desired. Clicking on the circled item in the toolbox will display these choices.

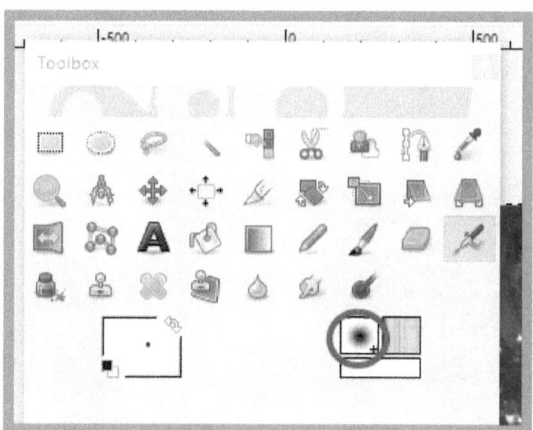

You have a wide range of choices.

Photo Phinishing

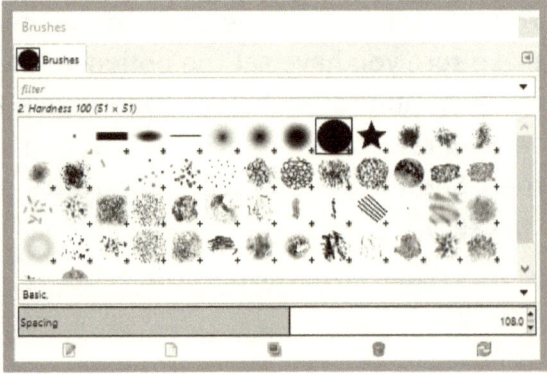

- Now use the airbrush tool on the areas to be modified. Repeat this for all the areas to be modified. You may want to enlarge the picture (as shown below) to make it easier to work with.

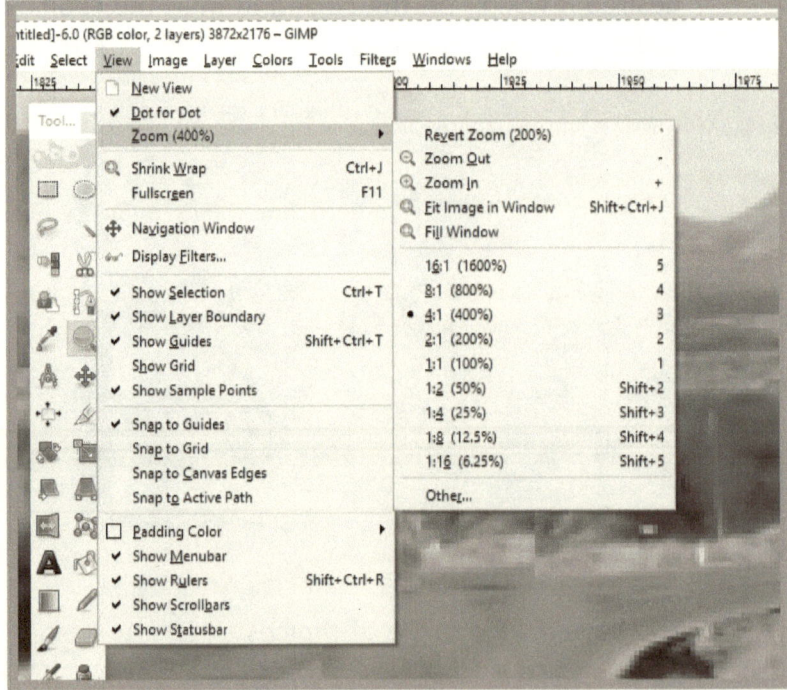

The airbrushed picture may look like this:

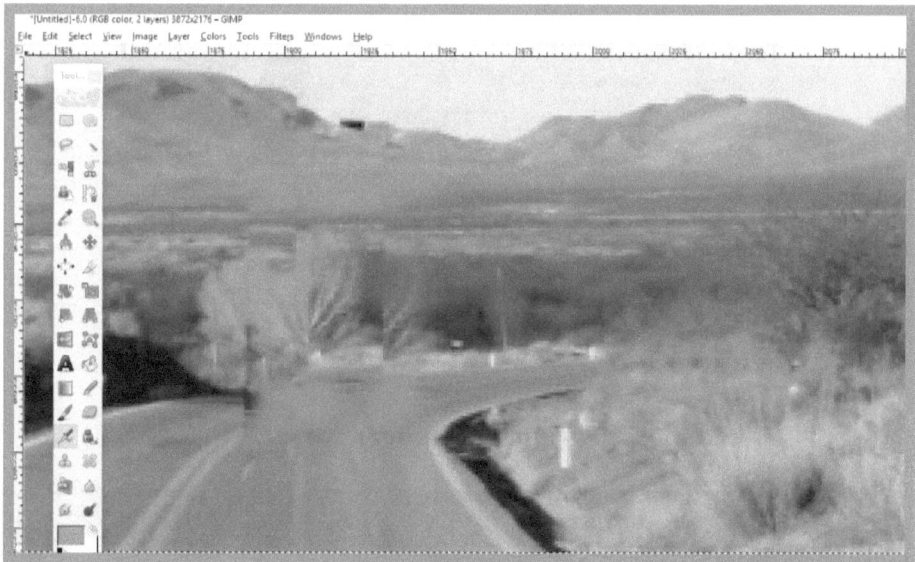

Appendix 4: Creating a Slideshow in PowerPoint

If you decide to use PowerPoint to create a slideshow from a set of pictures, there is an easy way to do this.

- Open PowerPoint with a new presentation or an existing one. Under the "INSERT" tab select "Photo Album" and "New Photo Album".

Photo Phinishing

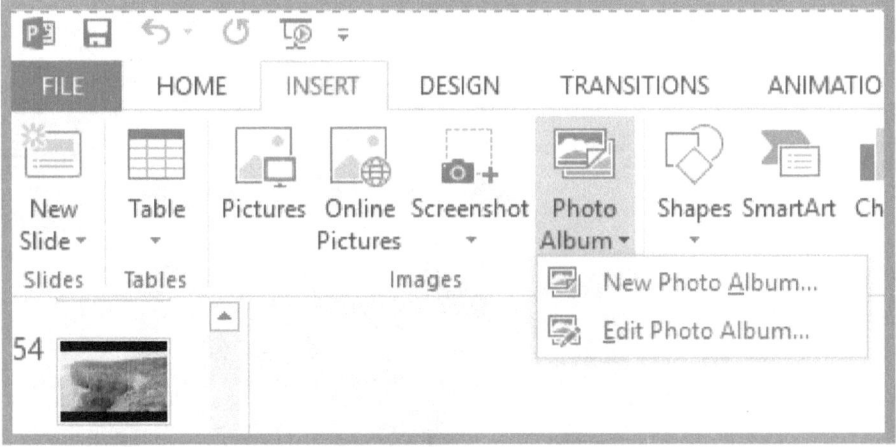

The following screen will appear.

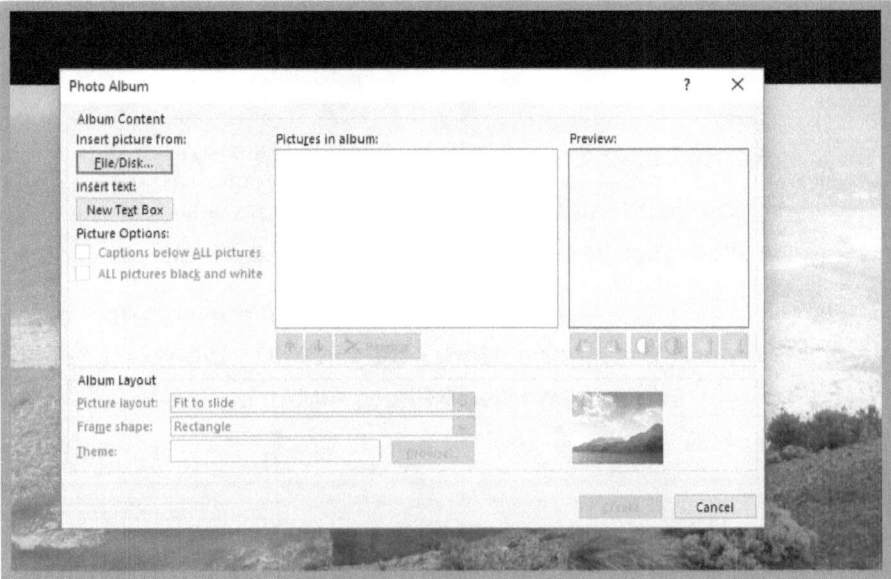

- Select "File/Disk". You will get an "Insert New Pictures" form.

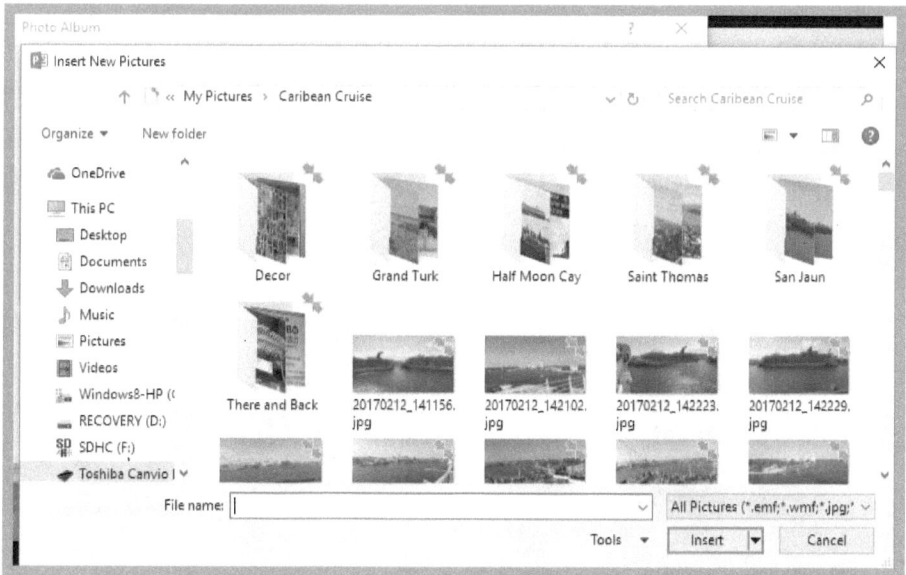

- Select the pictures you want to use, and press insert. You will get a screen like the following.

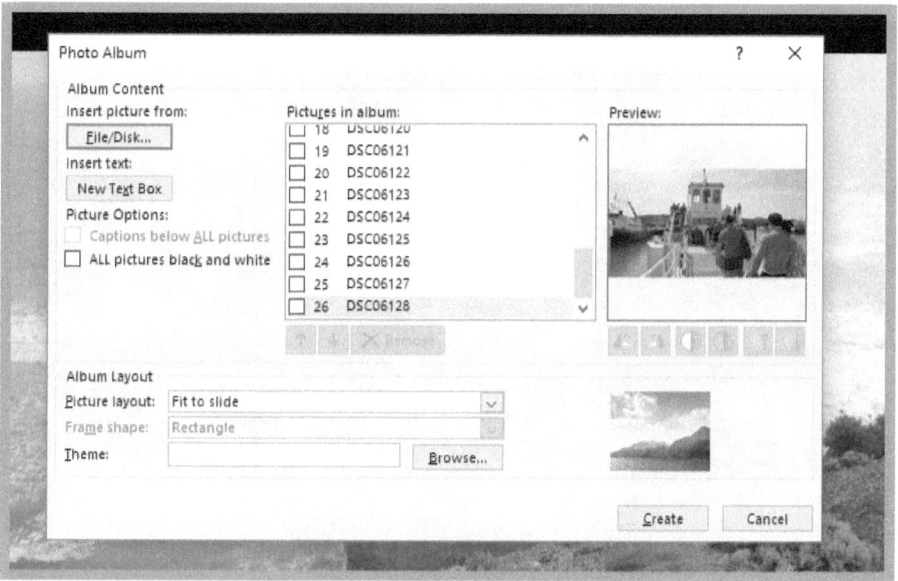

Photo Phinishing

- Press "Create" to create your slideshow (It may take a while.)

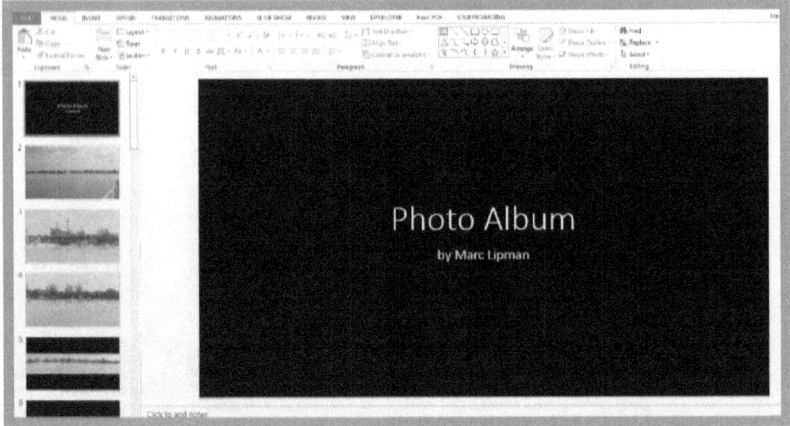

You can edit it as desired. Usually the first step is to change the text on the first slide and add a background picture. Setting its transparency to 50% is a good way to make the text easy to read.

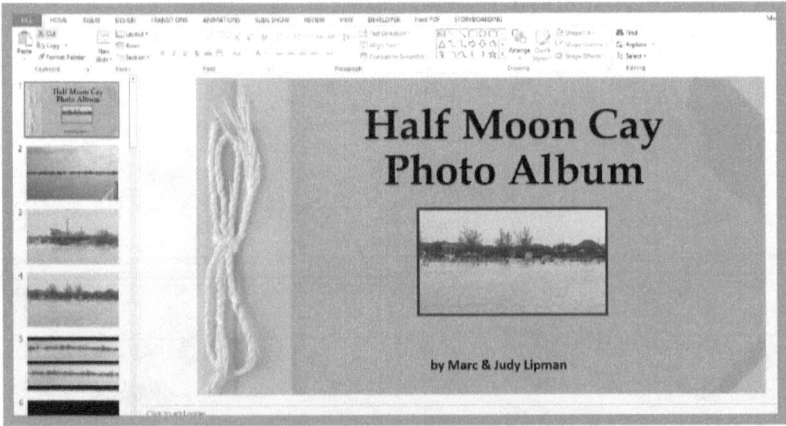

Now you can work with the organization and content of the picture slides as desired.

Marc Lipman

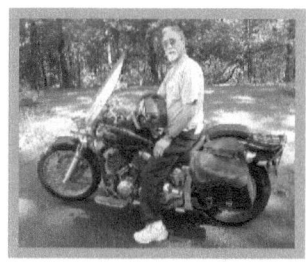

About the Author

Marc Lipman was born at an early age near Pennington, New Jersey and spent the first ten years of his life on a chicken farm there. It was a nice experience, but he realized it was not the career for him. His family later moved to Hackettstown, New Jersey where he graduated from Hackettstown High School. He went to Rutgers University and graduated with a degree in Electrical Engineering. He later got a masters degree in Computer Science from Stevens Institute of Technology.

Marc Lipman spent his career in the field of computers – having seen them grow (shrink) from multimillion-dollar room sized devices to handheld ones of equivalent power, occasionally teaching at the college and corporate level.

As some men do at a certain age, he developed a yen to own a motorcycle, and he bought one (his age was seventeen). Since then, he has owned ten of them.

As a sidelight he occasionally wrote items for publication in publications ranging from "Commodore" magazine to "Bridge" magazine. He still writes. He is a frequent contributor to the Sandpaper, the weekly newspaper for Long Beach Island.

Photo Phinishing

After "retiring", he pursued a number of hobbies and activities ranging from kayaking to duplicate bridge to softball to being a grandfather. He is currently an adjunct professor at a county college and a docent at the Barnegat Light Schoolhouse Museum.

I wish to thank Lauren Lipman (my daughter-in-law) for her extensive work in editing this document and making important suggestions!

4/9/2020

Marc Lipman

Other books by Marc Lipman*

Fiction

The Sandpaper Stories

Power to The People

And Now for Something Completely Different

The Bots Collection and Other Stories

Non-Fiction

CSC-105 BC

* Also available as E-Books